# Interactive
# Homework
## Workbook

Kindergarten

Scott Foresman · Addison Wesley

# en**Vision**MATH™

**Scott Foresman**
is an imprint of

pearsonschool.com

**Editorial Offices:** Glenview, Illinois • Parsippany, New Jersey • New York, New York
**Sales Offices:** Boston, Massachusetts • Duluth, Georgia • Glenview, Illinois
Coppell, Texas • Sacramento, California • Mesa, Arizona

ISBN-13: 978-0-328-34173-3

ISBN-10: 0-328-34173-8

18  VON4  15

# Contents

# Same and Different

**1**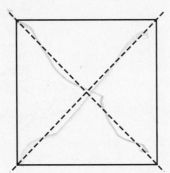

**2**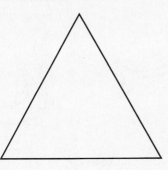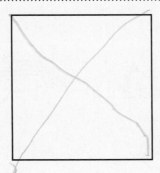

**3**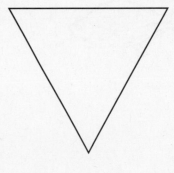

**4**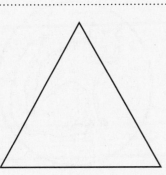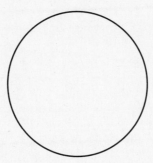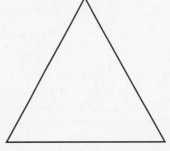

**Directions** Have children color the same two items in each row the same color. Have them mark an X on the item in each row that is different from the other two items.

1

# Sorting by One Attribute

**Directions** Have children sort the cats and the fish by drawing lines to the appropriate circles.

Name _____

# Sorting the Same Set in Different Ways

⭐ 1

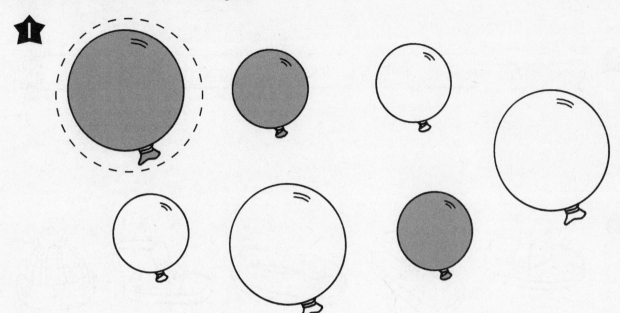

❷

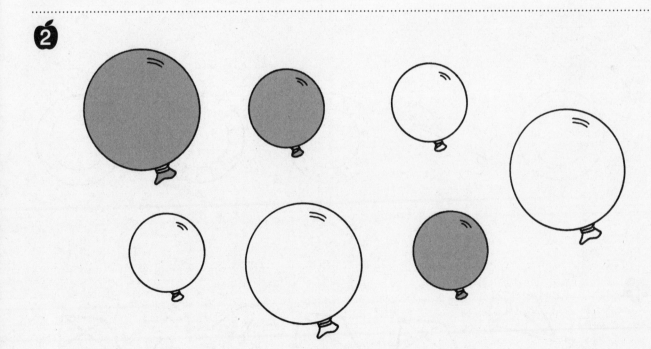

**Directions** Have children: ⭐ sort the balloons by circling all the large balloons; ❷ sort the balloons by circling all the shaded balloons.

**3**

# Sorting By More Than One
# Attribute

  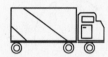  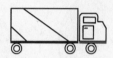 

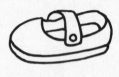    

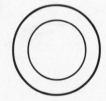  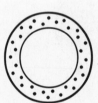 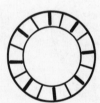 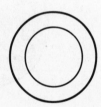

**Directions** Have children look at the objects in each row and mark an X on the object that doesn't belong.

4

Name _____

# Problem Solving: Use Logical Reasoning

 **1**

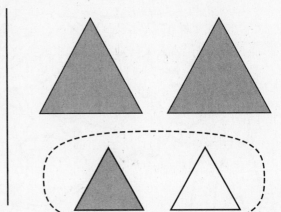

 **2**

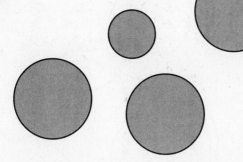

 **3**

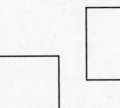 

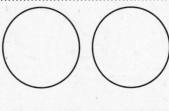

**Directions** For each exercise, have children identify how the attribute blocks are sorted on the left and circle the blocks at right that show the sorting rule.

5

# Inside and Outside

**Directions** Have children circle the bear and the rabbit outside the wagon. Have them circle the dog and the fish inside the wagon.

Name _____

# Over, Under, and On

**Directions** Have children mark an X on the cat and the bird on the chair, the mouse under the chair, and the spider over the chair.

7

# Top, Middle, and Bottom

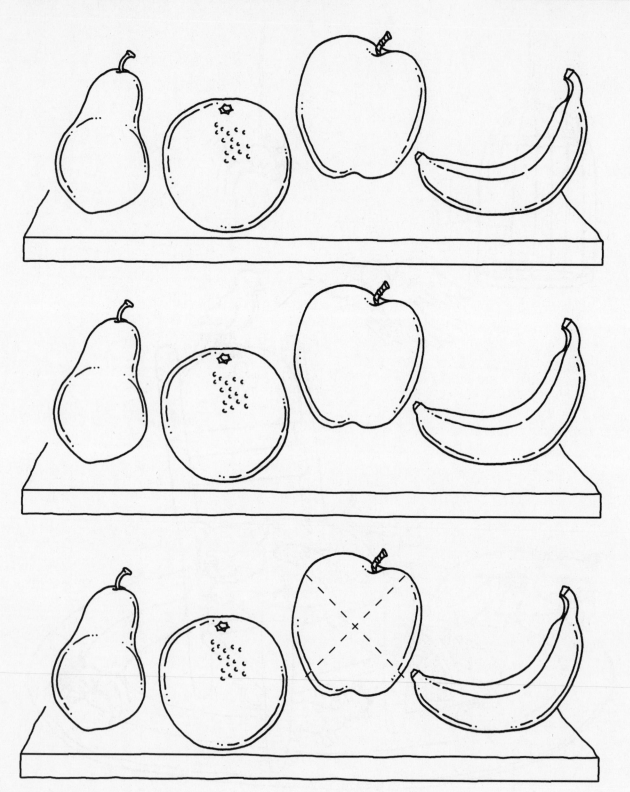

**Directions** Have children mark an X on the apple on the bottom, the orange on the top, and the banana in the middle.

# Before and After

 **1**

 **2**

**3**

 **4**

**Directions** Have children: **1** draw a carrot before the rabbit; **2** draw a carrot after the rabbit; **3** draw a worm before the bird; **4** draw a worm after the bird.

# Left and Right

## Left          ## Right

**Directions** Have children color the bird on the right blue, the puppy on the left brown, the fish on the right orange, and the kitten on the left yellow.

**10**

# Problem Solving: Act It Out

**Directions** *Marco wants to find the middle cloud. How can he find it? Place a counter on the left cloud. Place a counter on the right cloud. Now color the middle cloud.* Have children do the same to find and color the middle bee.

11

# Sound and Movement Patterns

   Peep

BAA

  Meow

ARF

**Directions** Have children: ❶–❷ draw a line to the picture of the animal that makes the next sound in the pattern; ❸–❹ circle the picture that comes next in the pattern.

# Comparing Patterns

 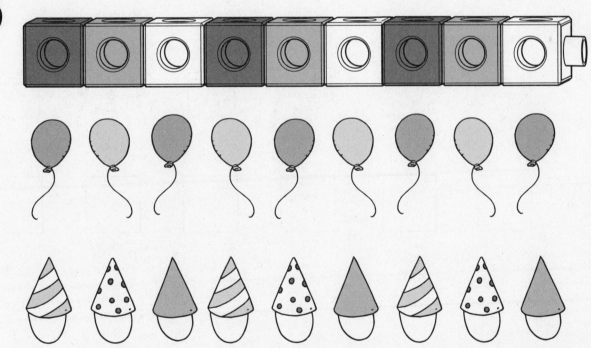

---

**Directions** Have children circle the pattern that matches the cube pattern at the top of each exercise.

# Problem Solving: Look for a Pattern

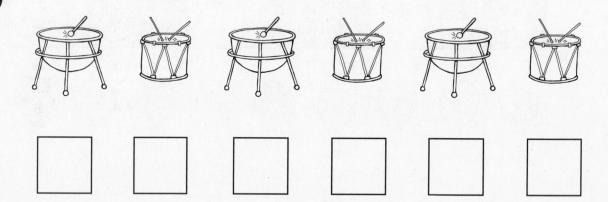

**Directions** For each exercise have children circle where the pattern repeats. Then have children show the pattern in another way by coloring the squares.

Name _____

# Using Patterns to Predict What Comes Next

 **1**

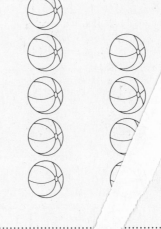

 **2**

**3**

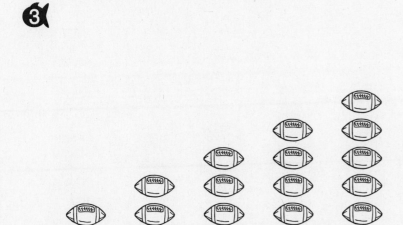

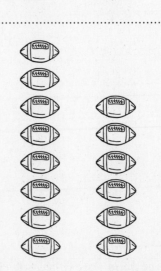

**Directions** Have children circle the set of pictures that shows what comes next in the pattern.

# Creating Patterns

 **1**

**2**

**3**

**Directions** Have children:  use two-color counters to make patterns and then color circles to match their patterns; **2** use two colors of tiles to make patterns and then color squares to match their patterns; **3** make patterns with counters and tiles and then draw and color the pattern.

# Counting 1, 2, and 3

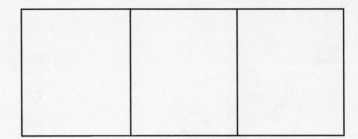

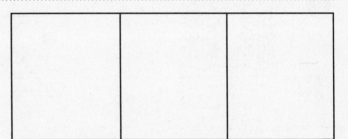

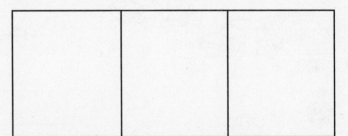

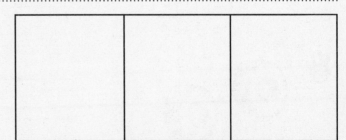

**Directions** Have children count the animals in each picture and color the correct number of boxes to show how many.

# Reading and Writing 1, 2, and 3

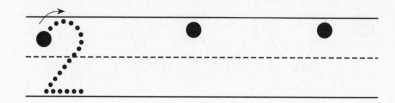

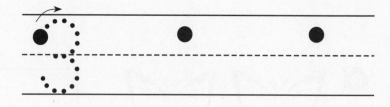

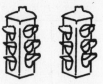

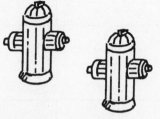

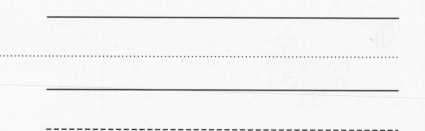

**Directions** Have children count each group and practice writing the number.

# Counting 4 and 5

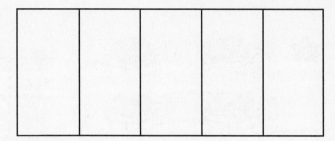

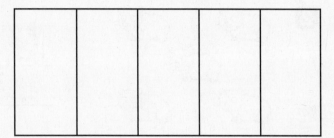

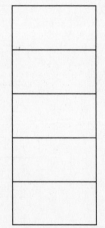

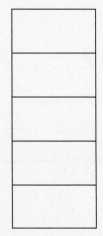

**Directions** Have children count the flowers in each group and color the correct number of boxes to show how many.

# Reading and Writing 4 and 5

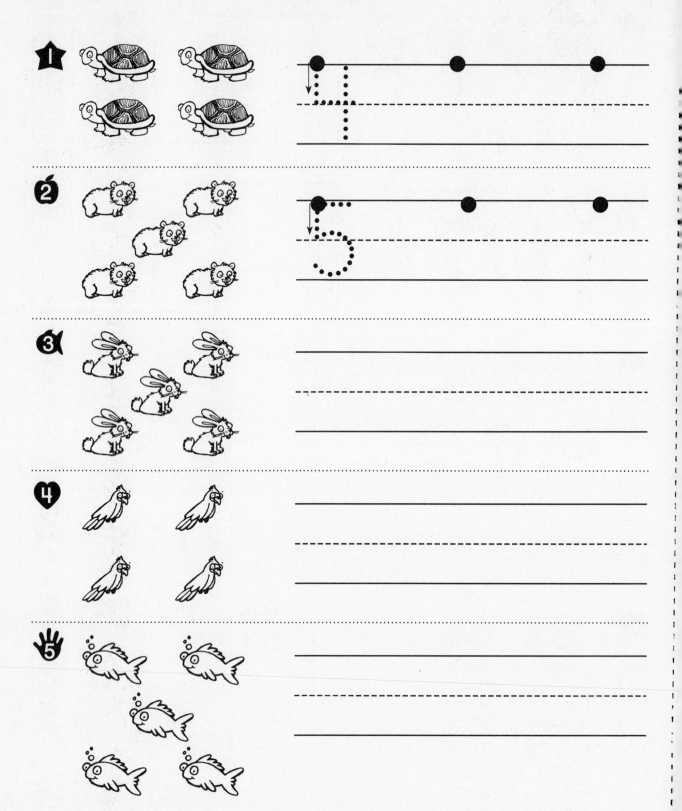

**Directions** Have children count each group and practice writing the number.

# Reading and Writing 0

  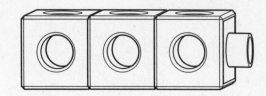

 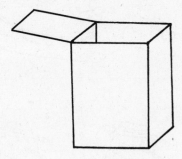 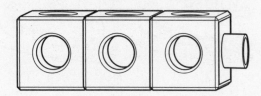

  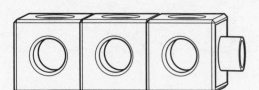

  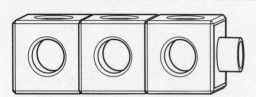

**Directions** Have children: ⭐ count the number of crayons in the box and color the cubes to tell how many; ❷ count the number of rulers in the box and color the cubes to tell how many; ❸ count the number of apples on the plate and color the cubes to tell how many; ❹ count the number of flowers in the vase and color the cubes to tell how many.

# Making 4 and 5

 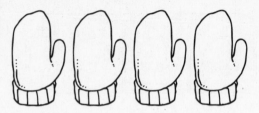

**Directions** Have children: ★-② color the objects with red and yellow crayons to show different ways to make 4; ③-✋ color the objects with red and yellow crayons to show different ways to make 5.

Name _____

# More, Fewer, and Same as

**★1**

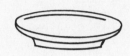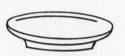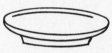

**❷2**

**❸3**

**♥4**

**Directions** Have children draw a line from each item in the top row to each item in the bottom row. Then circle each group that has fewer.

# I and 2 More

 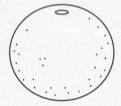 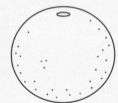 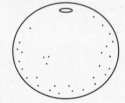

**Directions** Have children draw 1 more banana, 1 more sandwich, 2 more oranges, and 2 more muffins. Then have children tell about each row of pictures using the words *1 more* or *2 more*.

# 1 and 2 Fewer

 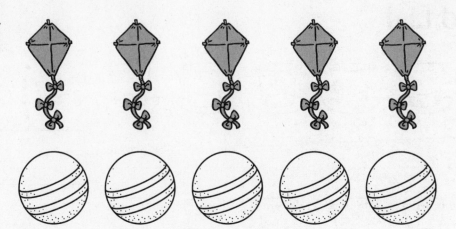

 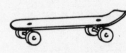 

**Directions** Have children look at the shaded objects and then color: ⭐ 2 fewer objects; 🍎 1 fewer object; ❸ 1 fewer object.

# Problem Solving: Make an Organized List

**Directions** Have children list numbers from 5 to 0 on the left and 0 to 5 on the right. Then have them show the different ways to make 5 by using blue and red crayons to color the hats that correspond with the numbers.

# Counting 6 and 7

 **1**

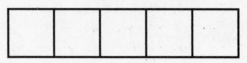

 **2**

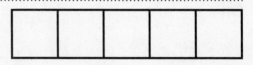

**3**

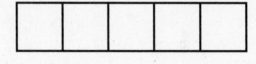

 **4**

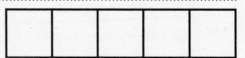

**Directions** Have children count the birds and then draw the correct number of counters to show how many.

# Making 6 and 7

⭐ **1**

🍎 **2**

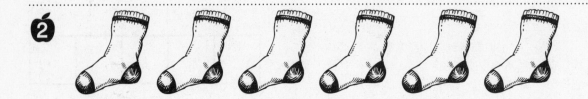

⭐ **3**

❤️ **4**

✋ **5**

**Directions** Have children: **1**–**3** color the clothes with red and yellow crayons to show different ways to make 6; **4**–**5** color the clothes with red and yellow crayons to show different ways to make 7.

# Reading and Writing 6 and 7

⭐ **1**

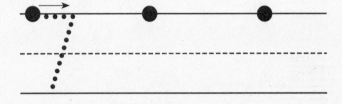

② **2**

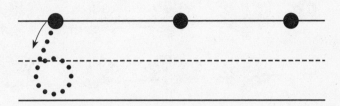

❸ **3**

_____

- - - - - - - - - - - - - - -

_____

❤ **4**

_____

- - - - - - - - - - - - - - -

_____

✋ **5**

_____

- - - - - - - - - - - - - - -

_____

---

**Directions** Have children count each group and practice writing the number.

# Counting 8 and 9

**1**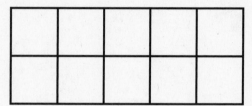

**2**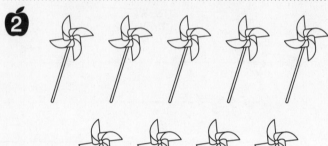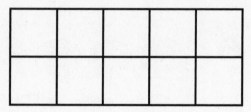

**3**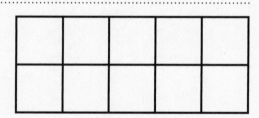

**4**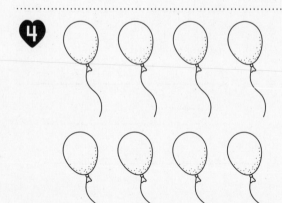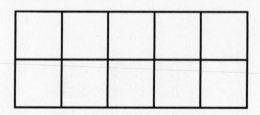

**Directions** Have children count the objects in each group and draw the correct number of counters to show how many.

Name _____

# Making 8 and 9

⭐ 1

🍎 2

🐟 3

❤️ 4

✋ 5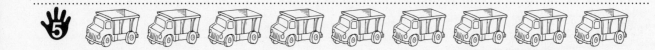

**Directions** Have children: ⭐–🍎 color the objects with red and yellow crayons to show different ways to make 8; 🐟–✋ color the objects with red and yellow crayons to show different ways to make 9.

# Reading and Writing 8 and 9

**1**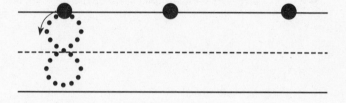

**2**

**3**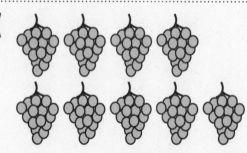

**4**

**5**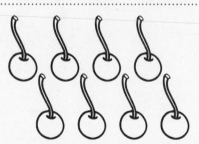

**Directions** Have children count each group and practice writing the number.

34

# Counting 10

**1**

**2**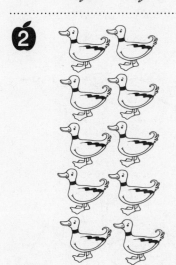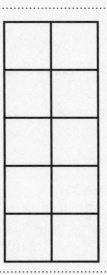

**3**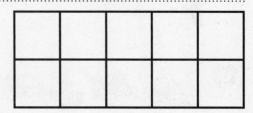

**4**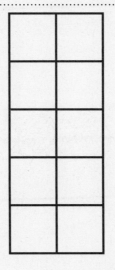

---

**Directions** Have children count the animals in each picture, and draw the correct number of counters to show how many.

# Making 10

**1**

**2**

**3**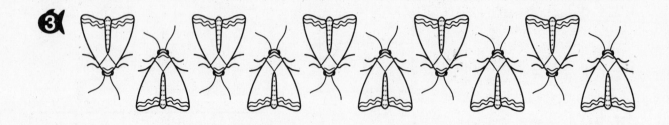

**4**

**5**

**Directions** Have children color each picture red or yellow to show different ways to make 10.

Name _____

# Reading and Writing 10

**1**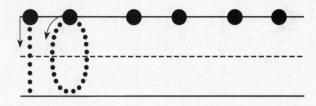

**2**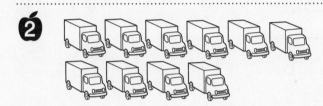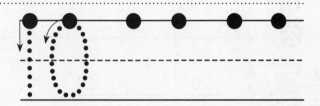

**3**

**4**

**Directions** Have children count the objects in each group and practice writing the number 10.

37

# Using a Number Line

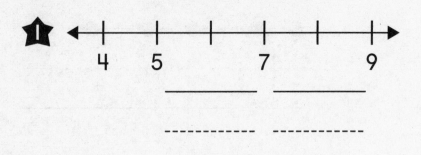

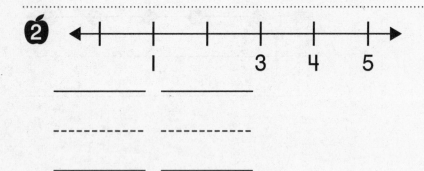

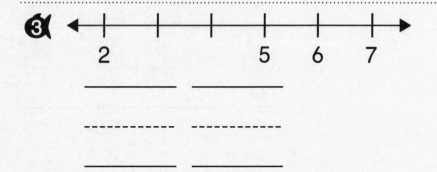

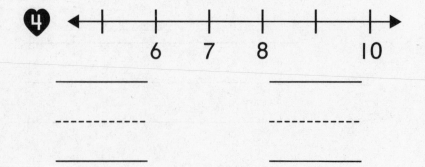

**Directions** Have children write the missing numbers in each number line.

# Problem Solving: Make a Graph

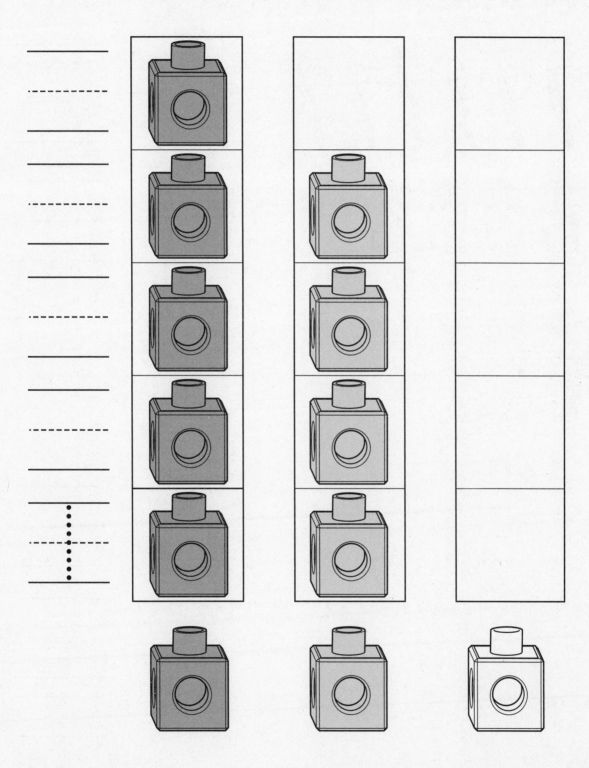

# Comparing Numbers Through 10

**1**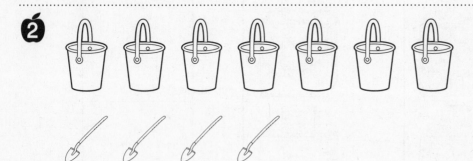

_____

_____

**2**

_____

_____

**3**

_____

_____

**4**

_____

_____

**Directions** Have children draw a line from each item in one group to each item in the other group. Then count and write the number and circle the lesser number.

**40**

# Comparing Numbers to 5

**1**

_____
- - - - - - - - - - -
_____

**2**

_____
- - - - - - - - - - -
_____

**3**

_____
- - - - - - - - - - -
_____

**4**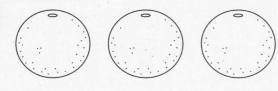

_____
- - - - - - - - - - -
_____

**Directions** Have children count how many and write the number. Then children circle the number if it is less than 5.

# Comparing Numbers to 10

 **1**

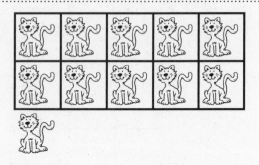 **2**

 **3**

 **4**

**5**

**Directions** Have children circle each picture that shows fewer than 10.

42

# 1 and 2 More and Fewer

 **1**

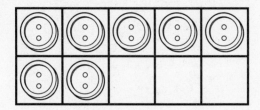

_____

- - - - - - - - - -

_____

**2**

_____

- - - - - - - - - -

_____

**3**

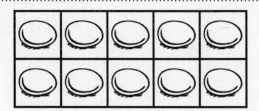

_____

- - - - - - - - - -

_____

**Directions** Have children: ⭐ draw a group that has 1 more object and then write the number that tells how many; ② draw a group that has 2 more objects and then write the number that tells how many; ③ draw a group that has 2 fewer objects and then write the number that tells how many.

**43**

# Problem Solving: Use Objects

_____

------------

_____

_____

------------

_____

_____

------------

_____

_____

------------

_____

_____

------------

_____

---

**Directions** *Nina sees butterflies in a bush. Then she sees 2 more. How many butterflies are there now?* Have children use counters and explain their answers. Then have them write the number.

# Squares and Other Rectangles

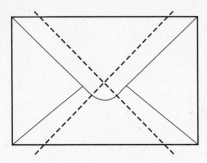  

 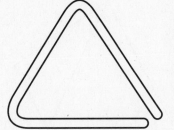 

**Directions** Have children: ❶-❷ mark an X on the objects that are shaped like a rectangle; ❸-❹ circle the objects that are shaped like a square.

Name _____

# Circles and Triangles

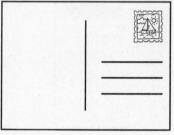

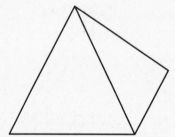

YIELD

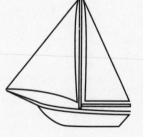

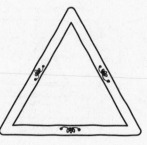

**Directions** Have children: ❶-❷ mark an X on the objects that are shaped like a circle; ❸-❹ circle the objects that are shaped like a triangle.

Name _____

# Making Shapes from Other Shapes

 **1** 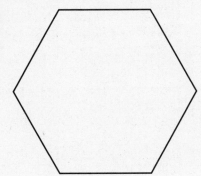 |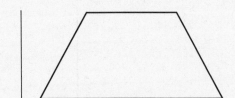

 **2** 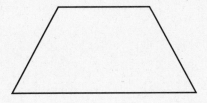 |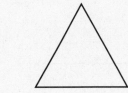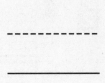

 **3** 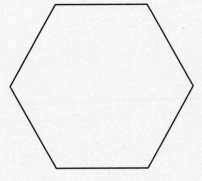 |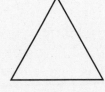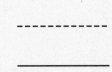

 **4**  |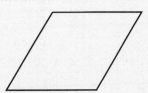

**Directions** Have children cover the shape with the type of pattern block that is shown. Then have them write the number of blocks that they used.

Name _____

# Same Size, Same Shape

 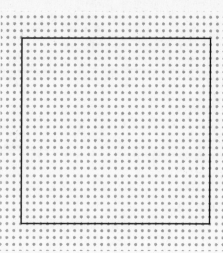

 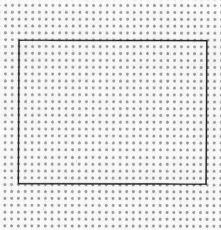

 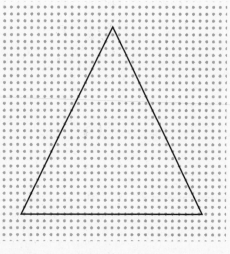

**Directions** Have children draw a figure that is the same size and shape.

# Name

# Symmetry

 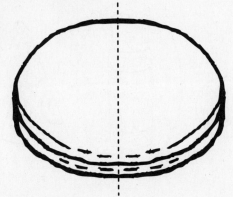

 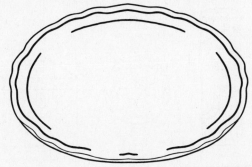

**Directions** Have children draw a line through each object to show matching parts.

# Solid Figures

**1**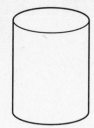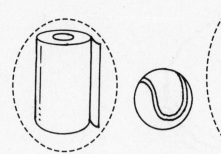

**2**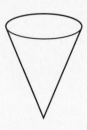

**3**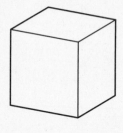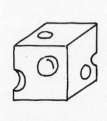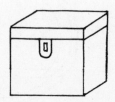

**4**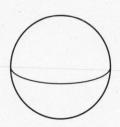

**Directions** In each row have children name the solid figure on the left. Then have children circle the objects on the right that have the same shape as the solid figure.

**50**

# Comparing Solid Figures

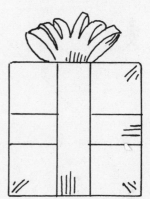

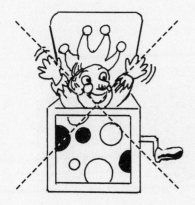

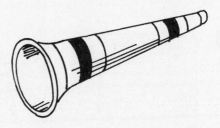

---

**Directions** Have children circle each item that can roll. Then have them mark an X on each item that can slide. Point out that some items that are circled should also be marked with an X.

# Flat Surfaces of Solid Figures

  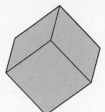  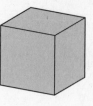 

 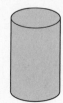  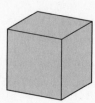

**Directions** In each exercise have children circle the solid figures with a flat surface that matches the shape on the left.

# Problem Solving: Use Objects

 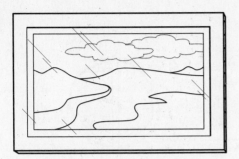

 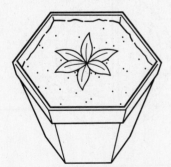

**Directions** Have children find the pattern block shape that matches the shape of each pictured object and then trace the pattern block shape. Then have them explain how they know that the shapes match.

Name _____

# Equal Parts

  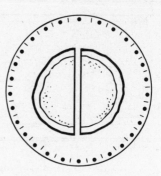

 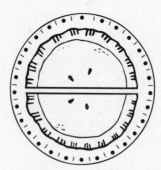 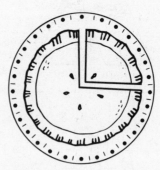

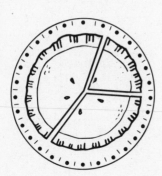  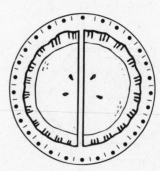

**Directions** Have children circle the items that are cut into equal parts in each row.

# Halves

 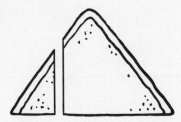 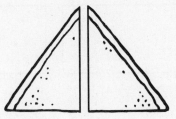 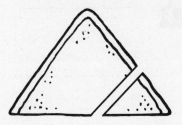

 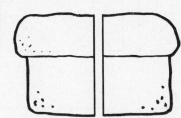 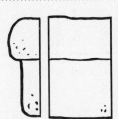 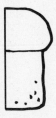 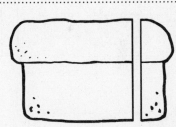

---

**Directions** Have children circle the picture that shows halves.

# Problem Solving: Act it Out

**1**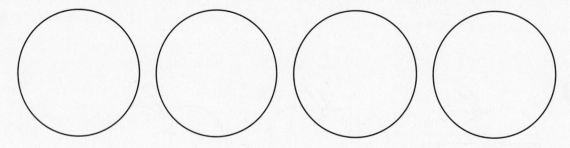

**2**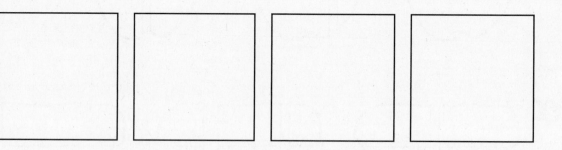

**3**

**4**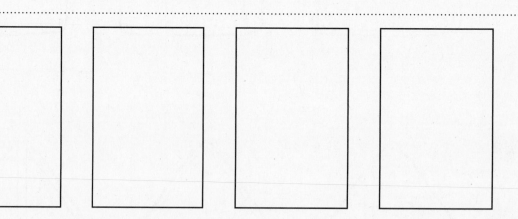

**Directions** In each row, have children draw a line on each shape to show how to make two equal parts four different ways.

56

# Ordinal Numbers Through Fifth

**1**

**2**

**3**

**4**

**5**

---

**Directions** Have children: **1** circle the first elephant; **2** circle the second elephant; **3** circle the third elephant; **4** circle the fourth elephant; **5** circle the fifth elephant. Check that children understand where each line begins and ends.

# Ordinal Numbers Through Tenth

**1**

**2**

**3**

**4**

**5**

**Directions** Have children: **1** circle the fifth dog; **2** circle the sixth mouse; **3** circle the seventh chick; **4** circle the eighth cat; **5** circle the tenth rabbit. Check that children understand where each line begins.

Name _____

# Problem Solving: Draw a Picture

---

**Directions** Have children trace the first hat in each row and then draw four more. Then have them use a yellow crayon and direct them to color in: ✦ the third cap; ② the first top hat; ③ the fifth helmet; ④ the second party hat. Then have children use other colors to fill in all the hats. Have them explain in which position each of their colors are.

# Comparing and Ordering
# by Size

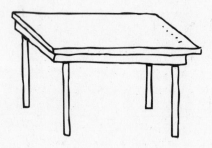  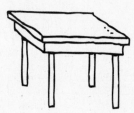

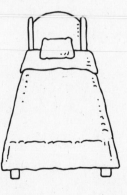 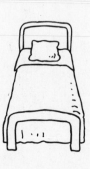 

**Directions** Have children order the objects in each exercise by circling the largest one, marking an X on the smallest one, and drawing a line under the medium-sized one.

# Comparing Lengths

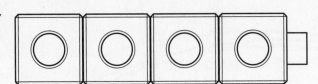

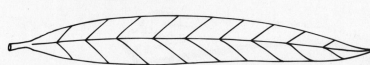
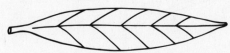

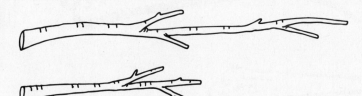

**Directions** Have children: ⭐ circle the object that is longer than the cube train; ❷ mark an X on the shorter branch; ❸ – ❹ circle the taller object and mark an X on the shorter object.

Name _____

# Ordering by Length

**1**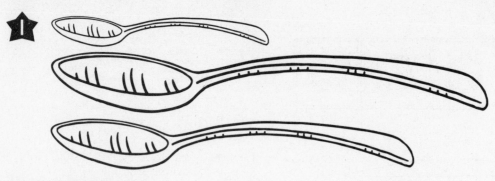

**2**

**3**

**Directions** Have children: **1** – **2** color the longest object blue and the shortest object red; **3** color the tallest object yellow and the shortest object green.

Name _____

# Measuring Length

 **1**

 **2**

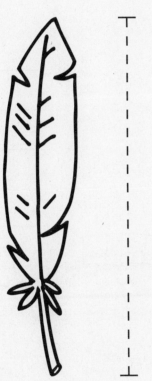 **3**

**4**

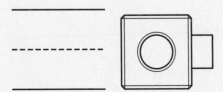

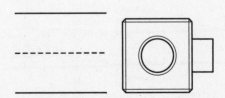

**Directions** Have children use cubes to measure each item and them write the number.

# Problem Solving: Try, Check, and Revise

_____

- - - - - - - - - - -

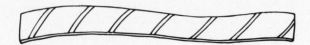

_____

- - - - - - - - - - -

_____

- - - - - - - - - - -

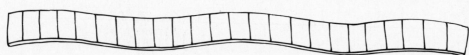

_____

- - - - - - - - - - -

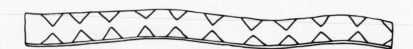

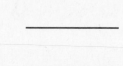

_____

- - - - - - - - - - -

**Directions** *Olivia wants to order pieces of ribbon from shortest to longest. How can we try to find out? How can we check and revise?* Have children compare and order the pieces of ribbon by writing 1 to 5 to show shortest to longest. Then have them discuss their results.

# Comparing Capacities

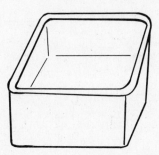

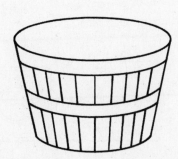

**Directions** Have children compare objects by drawing a line from the object on the left that holds less to the matching object on the right that holds more.

Name _____

# Measuring Capacity

**1**

_ _ _ _ _ _ _ _ _ _ _ _ _ _ _ _ _ _ _ _

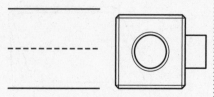

**2**

_ _ _ _ _ _ _ _ _ _ _ _ _ _ _ _ _ _ _ _

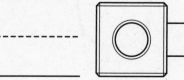

**3**

_ _ _ _ _ _ _ _ _ _ _ _ _ _ _ _ _ _ _ _

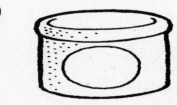

**4**

_ _ _ _ _ _ _ _ _ _ _ _ _ _ _ _ _ _ _ _

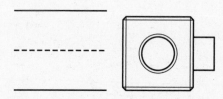

**5**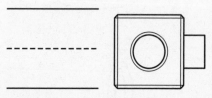

_ _ _ _ _ _ _ _ _ _ _ _ _ _ _ _ _ _ _ _

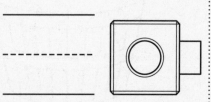

**6**

_ _ _ _ _ _ _ _ _ _ _ _ _ _ _ _ _ _ _ _

**Directions** Provide small containers similar to those pictured. Have children measure by filling each container with cubes. Then have them record the number to show the capacity.

66

Name _____

# Comparing Weights

 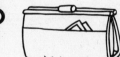 

**Directions** Have children: ★–❹ circle the heavier object, ✋–❻ mark an X on the lighter object.

Name _____

# Measuring Weight

 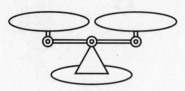 _____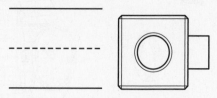

 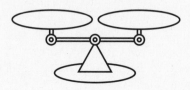 _____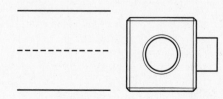

 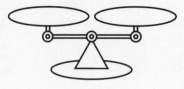 _____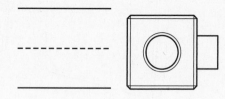

 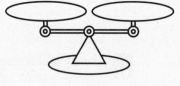 _____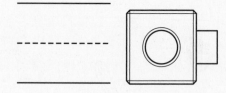

 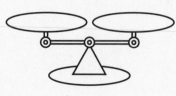 _____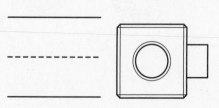

**Directions** Provide small objects similar to those pictured. Have children use a balance scale to weigh each object and record the number of cubes.

68

Name _____

# Problem Solving: Try, Check, and Revise

**1**

_____

- - - - - - - -

_____

 **2**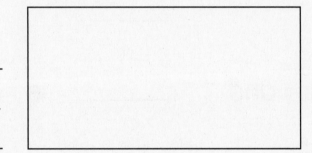

_____

- - - - - - - -

_____

**3**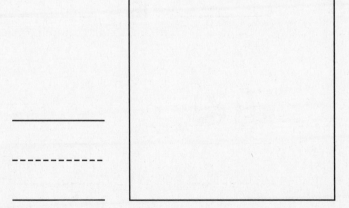

_____

- - - - - - - -

_____

**Directions** *Ms. Chun wants to put tiles on the top of each jewelry box. How many tiles does she need to cover each box? How can we use tiles to estimate and check?* Have children estimate and record the number on the left. Then children cover the boxes with tiles, count, and record their findings at right. Discuss the estimates and results.

# Stories About Joining

_____     _____     _____

- - - - - - - - -     - - - - - - - - -     - - - - - - - - -

_____ and _____ is _____.

_____                    _____

- - - - - - - - -     - - - - - - - - -     - - - - - - - - -

_____ and _____ is _____.

_____     _____     _____

- - - - - - - - -     - - - - - - - - -     - - - - - - - - -

_____ and _____ is _____.

_____                    _____

- - - - - - - - -     - - - - - - - - -     - - - - - - - - -

_____ and _____ is _____.

**Directions** Have children listen to each number story. Then write a number sentence that tells the story.  *Rebecca finds 1 red marble. Then she finds 3 blue marbles. How many marbles are there in all?* ❷ *Billy picks up 4 pine cones. Then he picks up 2 more. How many pinecones are there in all?* ❸ *Rob saw 3 brown leaves. Then he saw 3 yellow leaves. How many leaves are there in all?* ❹ *Jill found 3 small bells. Then she found 2 large bells. How many bells are there in all?*

# More Joining

_____        _____        _____

- - - - - - -        - - - - - - -        - - - - - - -

_____ and _____ is _____  .

**2**

_____        _____        _____

- - - - - - -        - - - - - - -        - - - - - - -

_____ and _____ is _____  .

**3**

_____        _____        _____

- - - - - - -        - - - - - - -        - - - - - - -

_____ and _____ is _____  .

**4**

_____        _____        _____

- - - - - - -        - - - - - - -        - - - - - - -

_____ and _____ is _____  .

**Directions** Have children write a number for each group. Then have them draw a circle to join the groups and write how many there are in all.

# Joining Groups

**1**   _____

**2**    _____

**3**    _____

**4**    _____

**5**

**Directions** Have children use cubes to show each group and then join the cubes. Then have them write the number that tells how many birds there are altogether.

# Using the Plus Sign

5        and        I

_____          _____

- - - - - - - -      - - - - - - - -

_____          _____

**2**

2        and        3

_____          _____

- - - - - - - -      - - - - - - - -

_____          _____

**3**

I        and        2

_____          _____

- - - - - - - -      - - - - - - - -

_____          _____

**Directions** Have children look at each picture. Then have them write numbers and a plus sign to show joining the groups.

# Finding Sums

------------   +   ------------   ::::   ------------

    5      and      5      is      10.

------------   +   ------------   ::::   ------------

    4      and      2      is      6.

------------   +   ------------   ::::   ------------

    3      and      6      is      9.

------------   +   ------------   ::::   ------------

    6      and      1      is      7.

**Directions** Have children trace the numbers to tell how many there are in each group. Have them circle the two groups to join them. Then have them trace the plus sign and equal sign and write the sum.

# Name _____

# Addition Sentences

 1.

_____ + _____ = _____

 2.

_____ + _____ = _____

3.

_____ + _____ = _____

  4.

_____ + _____ = _____

 5.

_____ + _____ = _____

**Directions** Have children write the numbers to tell how many there are in each group. Have them circle the two groups to join them. Then have them trace the plus sign and equals sign and write the sum.

Name _____

# Problem Solving: Draw a Picture

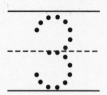 +  =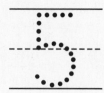

❷

——— + ——— = ———

❸

——— + ——— = ———

**Directions** Have children listen to these problems and then draw pictures to solve them. Then have children write
the numbers that tell about the picture. ❶ *Julia has 3 red balls and 2 green balls. How many balls does she have
altogether?* ❷ *Luis has 4 yellow balls and 2 red balls. How many balls does he have altogether?* ❸ *Sean has 5 black
balls and 1 red ball. How many balls does he have altogether?*

**76**

# Stories About Separating

_____
- - - - - - - - - -
_____  are left.

_____
- - - - - - - - - -
_____  are left.

_____
- - - - - - - - - -
_____  are left.

**Directions** Have children listen to each number story and count how many are left. Then they write the number.
⭐ *Kate sees 6 ducks. 3 ducks fly away. How many ducks are left?* ❷ *Ted sees 6 frogs. 1 frog hops away. How many frogs are left?* ❸ *Lori sees 6 chipmunks. 2 run away. How many are left?*

# Stories About Take Away

 **1**

_____  _____  _____  _____  _____

- - - - - - - - - - - -         - - - - - - - - - - - -     - - - - - - - - - -

_____ take away _____ is _____ .

 **2**

_____  _____  _____  _____  _____  _____

- - - - - - - - - - - -         - - - - - - - - - - - -     - - - - - - - - - -

_____ take away _____ is _____ .

 **3**

_____  _____  _____  _____  _____  _____  _____  _____

- - - - - - - - - - - -         - - - - - - - - - - - -     - - - - - - - - - -

_____ take away _____ is _____ .

**Directions** Have children listen to each number story. Have them count and record the number in all. Ask them to trace or mark Xs to show how many to take away and record this number. Then have children write the number that tells how many are left. **1** *Eric sees 5 geese. Three geese fly away. How many geese are left?* **2** *Eric sees 6 chicks. One chick walks away. How many chicks are left?* **3** *Eric sees 8 ducklings. Three swim away. How many ducklings are left?*

# Stories About Comparing

**1**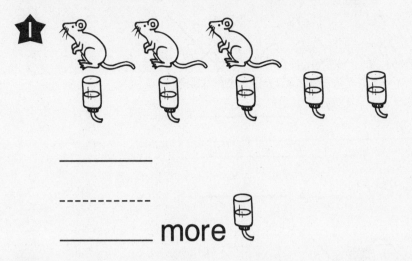

_____

- - - - - - - - -

_____ more 🔔

**2**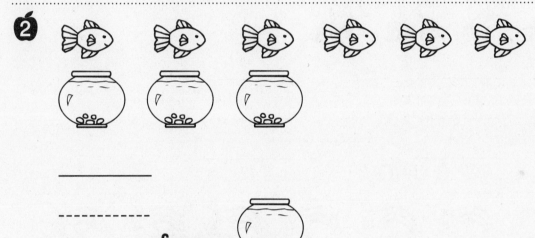

_____

- - - - - - - - -

_____ fewer 🐟

**3**

_____

- - - - - - -

_____ more 🥕

---

**Directions** Have children listen to each story to find out which group has more or fewer objects. Then they write how many more or fewer. **1** *There are 3 mice and 5 water containers. Are there more mice or water containers? How many more?* **2** *There are 6 fish and 3 bowls. Are there fewer fish or bowls? How many fewer?* **3** *There are 4 horses and 5 carrots. Are there more horses or carrots? How many more?*

# Using the Minus Sign

_____     • • • • • •     _____

- - - - - - - - - - -     • • • • •     - - - - - - - - - - -

_____                     _____

_____     • • • • • •     _____

- - - - - - - - - - -     • • • • •     - - - - - - - - - - -

_____                     _____

_____     • • • • • •     _____

- - - - - - - - - - -     • • • • •     - - - - - - - - - - -

_____                     _____

**Directions** Have children write how many animals there are in all. Have them trace Xs to subtract. Then have them trace the minus sign, write the number subtracted, and tell how many animals are left.

**Name** _____

# Finding Differences

 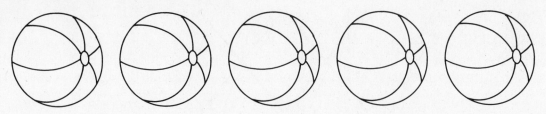

5    take away    2    is    3.
____         ____       ____

- - - - - - - -    .......    - - - - - - - -    :::::    - - - - - - -

____         ____       ____

**2**

6    take away    4    is    2.
____         ____       ____

- - - - - - - -    .......    - - - - - - - -    :::::    - - - - - - -

____         ____       ____

**3**

7    take away    I    is    6.
____         ____       ____

- - - - - - - -    .......    - - - - - - - -    :::::    - - - - - - -

____         ____       ____

**Directions** Have children write how many balls there are in all. Have them mark Xs to subtract. Ask children to trace the minus sign and write the number subtracted. Then have them trace the equal sign and write the difference.

Name _____

# Subtraction Sentences

_____    _____    _____

- - - - - - - - -    ......    - - - - - - - - -    ::::::    - - - - - - - - -

_____    _____    _____

_____    _____    _____

- - - - - - - - -    ......    - - - - - - - - -    ::::::    - - - - - - - - -

_____    _____    _____

 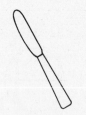    

_____    _____    _____

- - - - - - - - -    ......    - - - - - - - - -    ::::::    - - - - - - - - -

_____    _____    _____

**Directions** Have children write how many utensils there are in all. Have them trace Xs to subtract. Ask them to trace the minus sign and write the number subtracted. Then have children complete the subtraction sentence by tracing the equal sign and writing the difference.

82

# Problem Solving: Act It Out

**1**

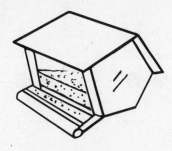

_____    _____    _____

- - - - - - - -        - - - - - - - -    _____ go.    - - - - - - - -

_____

**2**

_____    _____    _____

- - - - - - - -        - - - - - - - -    _____ go.    - - - - - - - -

_____

**3**

_____    _____    _____

- - - - - - - -        - - - - - - - -    _____ go.    - - - - - - - -

_____

**Directions** Have children listen as you tell a problem about each picture. Tell them to solve each problem by acting it out with counters. Have children write each answer.

# Counting, Reading, and Writing 11 and 12

**1**

**2**
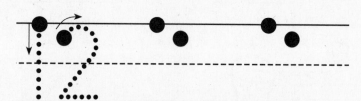

**3**

**4**

**Directions** Have children count each group and practice writing the numbers.

# Counting, Reading, and Writing
## 13, 14, and 15

**1**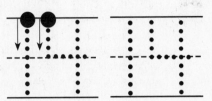

**2**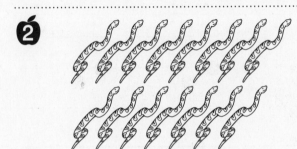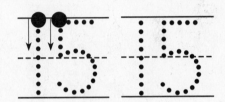

**3**

**4**

**5**

**Directions** In each row have children count the animals and practice writing the numbers.

# Counting, Reading, and Writing
## 16 and 17

⭐**1**
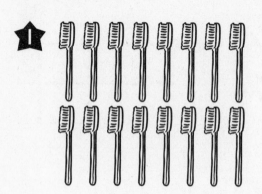
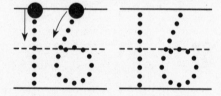

**2**
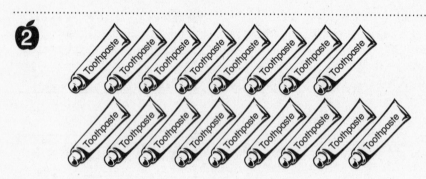
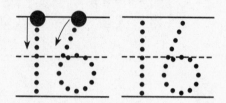

**3**
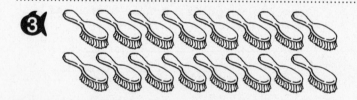
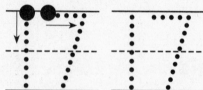

**4**
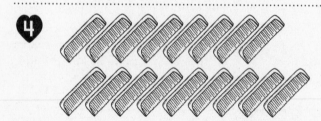
_____  _____
- - - - - - - -   - - - - - - - -
_____  _____

**5**

_____  _____
- - - - - - - -   - - - - - - - -
_____  _____

**Directions** In each row have children count the objects and practice writing the numbers.

**Name** _____

# Counting, Reading, and Writing 18, 19, and 20

**1**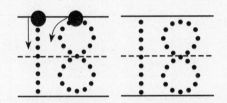

**2**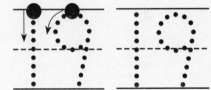

**3**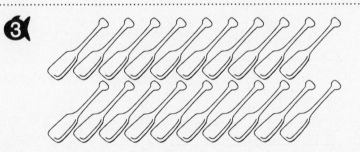

**4**

_____  _____

_ _ _ _ _ _ _ _  _ _ _ _ _ _ _ _

_____  _____

**5**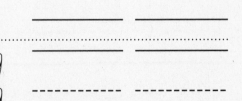

_____  _____

_ _ _ _ _ _ _ _  _ _ _ _ _ _ _ _

_____  _____

---

**Directions** In each row have children count the objects and practice writing the numbers.

87

# Odd and Even

_____

- - - - - - - - - - -

_____


❷

_____

- - - - - - - - - - -

_____

**Directions** Have children: ⭐ color the same number of squares in both rows, write the number that tells how many squares are colored, and explain why it is even; ❷ color the squares to show an odd number, write the number that tells how many squares are colored, and explain why it is odd.

88

Name _____

# Counting to 100

| 1 | 2 | 3 | 4 | 5 | 6 | 7 | 8 | 9 | 10 |
|---|---|---|---|---|---|---|---|---|---|
| 11 | 12 | 13 | 14 | 15 | 16 | 17 | 18 | 19 | 20 |
| 21 | 22 | 23 | | 25 | 26 | | 28 | 29 | 30 |
| | 32 | 33 | 34 | 35 | 36 | 37 | 38 | | 40 |
| 41 | | 43 | 44 | 45 | | 47 | 48 | 49 | 50 |
| 51 | 52 | | 54 | | 56 | 57 | 58 | 59 | 60 |
| 61 | | 63 | 64 | 65 | 66 | 67 | 68 | 69 | |
| 71 | 72 | | | 75 | 76 | 77 | 78 | 79 | 80 |
| 81 | 82 | 83 | 84 | | | 87 | 88 | 89 | 90 |
| 91 | | 93 | 94 | 95 | 96 | 97 | | 99 | 100 |

**Directions** Have children count to 100 on the hundred chart and write the missing numbers.

# Counting Groups of Ten

**1**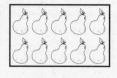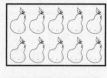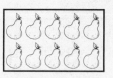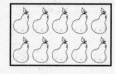

10    20    _____    _____    _____

**2**

10    _____    _____    _____    _____

**3**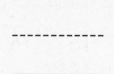

_____    20    _____    _____    _____

**Directions** In each exercise have children count the groups of 10 and write the numbers.

# Patterns on a Hundred Chart

| 1 | 2 | 3 | 4 | 5 | 6 | 7 | 8 | 9 | 10 |
|---|---|---|---|---|---|---|---|---|---|
| 11 | 12 | 13 | 14 | 15 | 16 | 17 | 18 | 19 | 20 |
| 21 | 22 | 23 | 24 | 25 | 26 | 27 | 28 | 29 | |
| 31 | 32 | 33 | 34 | 35 | 36 | 37 | 38 | 39 | |
| 41 | 42 | 43 | 44 | 45 | 46 | 47 | 48 | 49 | |
| 51 | 52 | 53 | 54 | 55 | 56 | 57 | 58 | 59 | |
| 61 | 62 | 63 | 64 | 65 | 66 | 67 | 68 | 69 | |
| 71 | 72 | 73 | 74 | 75 | 76 | 77 | 78 | 79 | |
| 81 | 82 | 83 | 84 | 85 | 86 | 87 | 88 | 89 | |
| 91 | 92 | 93 | 94 | 95 | 96 | 97 | 98 | 99 | |

**Directions** Have children count by 10s on the hundred chart and write the numbers. Then have children count by 5s and use a red crayon to circle the numbers they counted.

# Skip Counting by 2 and 5

0   2   4   6   8   10   12   14   16   18   20

 **1**

2   4   _____   _____   10

  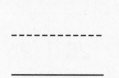  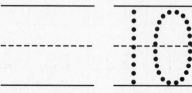

_____   14   _____   18   _____

    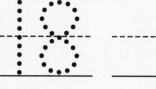

0 ······· 5 ······· 10 ······· 15 ······· 20

 **2**

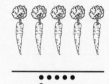 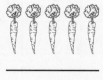 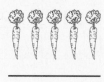

5   10   _____   _____

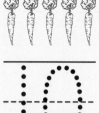 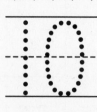

**3**

_____   _____   _____   _____

_____   _____   _____   _____

**Directions** Have children: ⭐ skip count by 2s to count the objects and record the numbers; ❷–❸ skip count by 5s and record the numbers.

# Problem Solving: Look for a Pattern

 | 18 | 17 | 16 | 15 | ------ | ------ |

**2** | 5 | 5 | 6 | 6 | ------ | ------ |

**3** | 9 | 9 | ------ | ------ | 11 | 11 |

**4** | 15 | 15 | ------ | ------ | 13 | 13 |

**Directions** *Look at each row of numbers. How can we find out the pattern?* Have children look at each row and decide the pattern and write the missing numbers.

# Penny

****

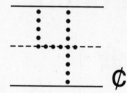

**②**

_____
------- ¢

**③**

_____
------- ¢

**④**

_____
------- ¢

**Directions** Have children count the pennies and write the correct value.

**Name** _____

# Nickel

       _____ 8 _____ ¢

---

**2**        _____ _____ ¢

---

**3**

    _____ _____ ¢

---

**4**

     _____ _____ ¢

---

**Directions** Have children find the value of each group of coins and write the number of cents.

**95**

Name _____

# Dime

_____
_____ ¢

_____
_____ ¢

_____
_____ ¢

_____
_____ ¢

**Directions** Have children find the value of each group of coins and write the number of cents.

96

Name _____

# Quarter and Dollar

  |

   |

   |

    |

**Directions** Have children identify the coins or bills on the left and circle the coin or bill on the right that belongs in the group.

# Comparing Money

**❶**

**❷**

**❸**

**❹**

**Directions** Have children mark an X on the item that costs *less* in each exercise.

**98**

# Problem Solving: Act It Out

 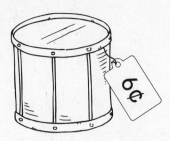

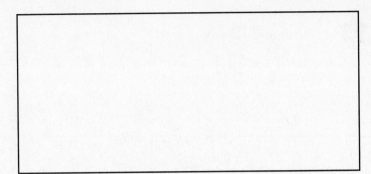

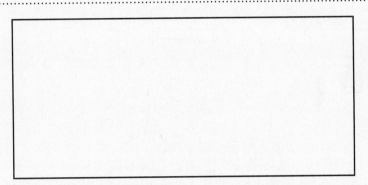

 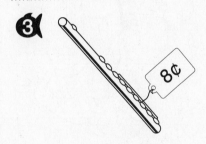

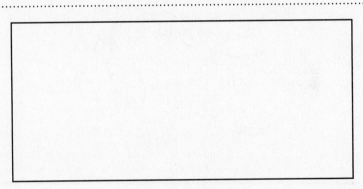

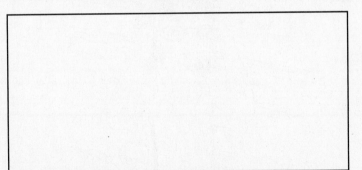

**Directions** Have children show the price of each item in different ways and then draw pictures of coins to show the price in one way.

# More Time and Less Time

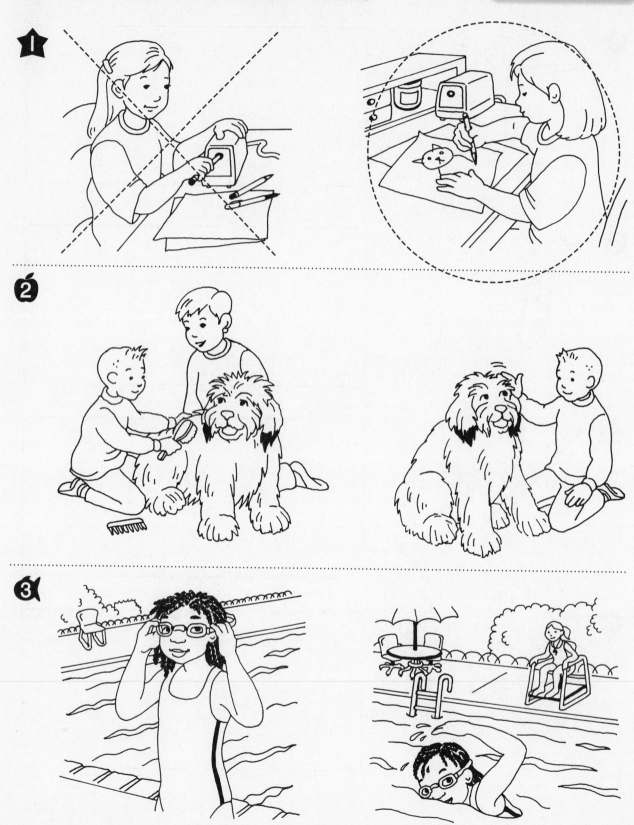

**Directions** In each exercise have children place an X on the event that takes less time and circle the event that takes more time.

# Order of the Day

 **1**

Morning

**2**

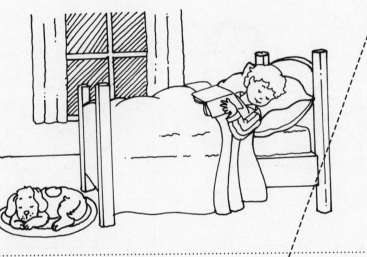

Afternoon

**3**

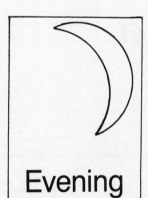

Evening

**Directions** In each exercise have children match the picture with the symbol for morning, afternoon, and evening.

Name _____

# Order of Events

_____  _____  _____

- - - - - - - -   - - - - - - - -   - - - - - - - -

_____  _____  _____

- - - - - - - -   - - - - - - - -   - - - - - - - -

**Directions** Have children: ① draw a line to the picture that shows what happens next; ②—③ order the events from first to last using the numbers 1, 2, and 3.

# Finding Numbers on Clocks

 **1**

**2**

**Directions** Have children trace the dotted numbers on the clocks.

# Telling Time to the Hour

 **1**

_____

_____

_____ o'clock

**2**

_____

_____

_____ o'clock

**3**

_____

_____

_____ o'clock

**4**

_____

_____

_____ o'clock

**Directions** Have children write the time to the hour that is shown on each clock.

# Times of Events

 **1**

_____
- - - - - - - - - - -
_____ o'clock

 **2**

_____
- - - - - - - - - -
_____ o'clock

 **3**

_____
- - - - - - - - - -
_____ o'clock

 **4**

_____
- - - - - - - - - -
_____ o'clock

**Directions** For each exercise, have children look at the clock and write the time to the hour for each activity. Have children circle the picture using a yellow crayon if it happens in the morning, a red crayon if it happens in the afternoon, and a blue crayon if it happens in the evening.

# Problem Solving: Use Logical Reasoning

**Directions** Have children: ⭐ color all the pictures that tell about a daytime activity; 🍎 color the pictures that tell about an evening activity.

# Months and Seasons

 **1**

January

February

March

April

May

June

July

August

September

October

November

December

**2**

Winter

Spring

Summer

Fall

**Directions** Have children: **1** circle the current month and mark an X on the last month of the year; **2** mark an X on the current season.

# Days of the Week

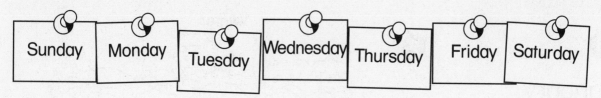

| Sunday | Monday | Tuesday | Wednesday | Thursday | Friday | Saturday |

| 1 | | Friday |

| 2 | | Tuesday |

| 3 | | Sunday |

| 4 | | Wednesday |

| 5 | | Saturday |

| 6 | | Monday |

| 7 | | Thursday |

**Directions** Have children put the days of the week in order by drawing a line to match each day with a number.

**108**

# Yesterday, Today, and Tomorrow

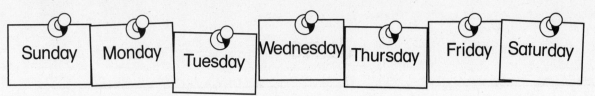

Sunday | Monday | Tuesday | Wednesday | Thursday | Friday | Saturday

## Today is

_____

- - - - - - - - - - - - - - - - - - - - - - - - - -

_____.

## Yesterday was

_____

- - - - - - - - - - - - - - - - - - - - - - - - - -

_____.

## Tomorrow will be

_____

- - - - - - - - - - - - - - - - - - - - - - - - - -

_____.

**Directions** Identify the day of the week for children. Read each sentence starter to them and have them complete each one by writing the corresponding day.

# Numbers on a Calendar

## June

| Sunday | Monday | Tuesday | Wednesday | Thursday | Friday | Saturday |
|--------|--------|---------|-----------|----------|--------|----------|
| | 1 | 2 | 3 | 4 | 5 | 6 |
| 7 | 8 | 9 | ___ | 11 | ___ | 13 |
| 14 | 15 | ___ | 17 | ___ | 19 | 20 |
| 21 | 22 | 23 | 24 | ___ | 26 | 27 |
| 28 | ___ | 30 | | | | |

**Directions** Have children trace or write the missing numbers.

# Calendar

| April | | | | | | |
|---|---|---|---|---|---|---|
| Sunday | Monday | Tuesday | Wednesday | Thursday | Friday | Saturday |
|  | 1 | 2 |  | 4 | 5 | 6 |
| 7 |  | 9 | 10 | 11 |  | 13 |
| 14 | 15 |  | 17 |  | 19 | 20 |
| 21 |  | 23 |  | 25 | 26 |  |
| 28 | 29 | 30 |  |  |  |  |

**Directions** Have children trace the name of the month and the dates on the calendar. Then have children fill in the missing dates and circle the names of the days of the week.

# Temperature

 **1**
 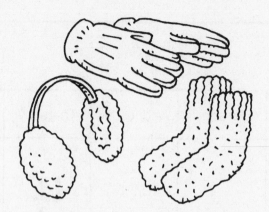 

 **2**

 **3**

**4**
 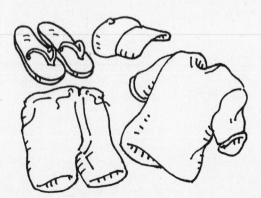 

**Directions** In each exercise have children circle the "hot thermometer" or the "cold thermometer" to show which goes with the items of clothing.

112

# Name _____

# Problem Solving: Draw a Picture

**Directions** *What can you draw on the children in each picture that goes with the scene?* Have children draw a picture to show what belongs in each scene. Then color each picture.

**113**

# As Many, More, and Fewer

 **1**

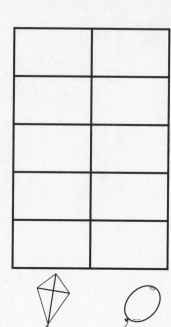

 **2**

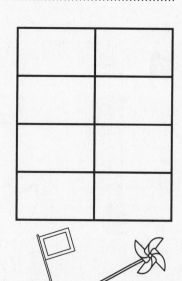

 **3**

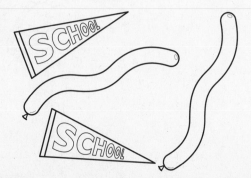

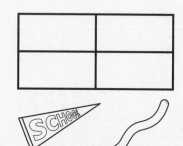

**Directions** Have children color a box on the graph for each object. Have them circle the picture above the column with fewer objects. If there is the same number of objects, circle the exercise number.

# Collecting Data

**1**
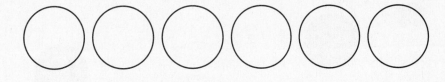

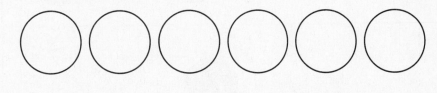

**2**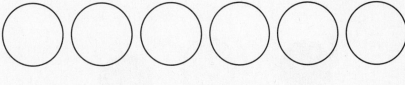
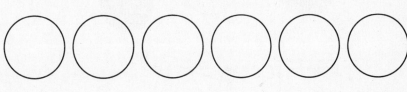

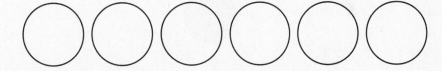

**3**
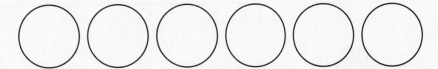
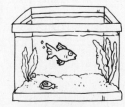
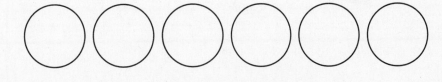

**4**

**Directions** For each pair of animals, have children survey a few classmates to see which pet they like better. Have them color a circle for each response. Then have children circle the pet in each pair that got the most votes.

Name _____

# Real Graphs

Name _____

Name _____

Name _____

Name _____

# Picture Graphs

**1**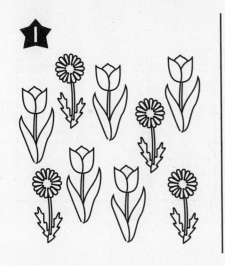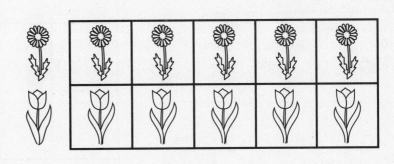

**2**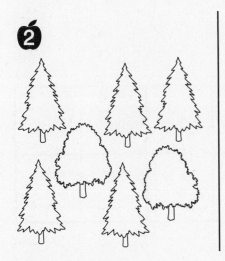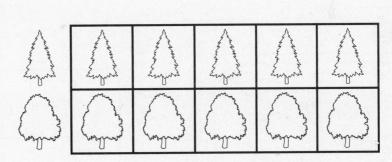

**3**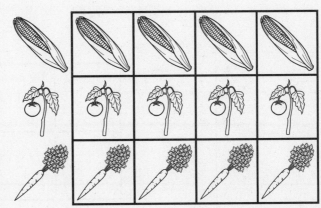

**Directions** Have children look at the objects in each picture and color a picture on the graph for each object. Then have them circle the row in each graph that has the most objects.

**117**

Name _____

# Bar Graphs

 **1**

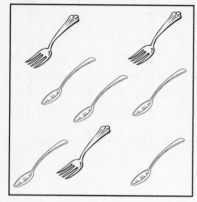    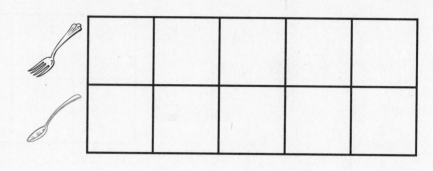

**2**

    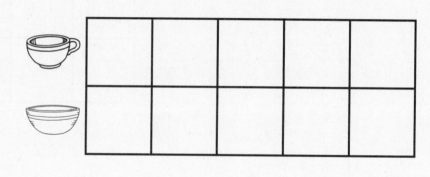

**3**

    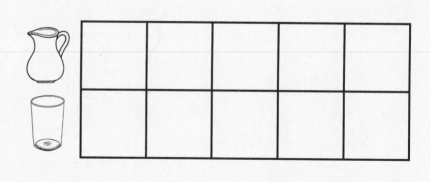

**Directions** For each exercise, have children color squares to show how many objects there are in each group.

# More Likely, Less Likely

 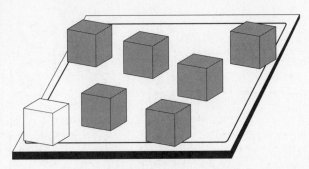 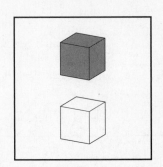

 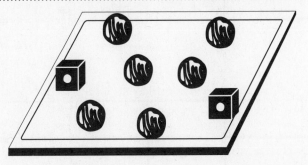 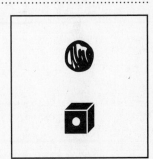

  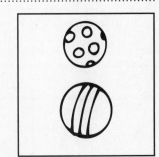

**Directions** Have children circle which object they would be *less likely* to take with their eyes closed.

# Problem Solving: Make a Graph

**Directions** Have children look at the picture and color a graph square for each giraffe, elephant, and gazelle on the zoo savannah. Then have them write the number of each animal and circle the label of the animal that indicates the fewest number.

**120**

© Pearson Education, Inc. K